We're Not OK

Jewish & Ally Experiences Post 10/7

Curated and Illustrated by Rachelle Gage

Dedicated to the victims, hostages, and
survivors of October 7th- and to the IDF
soldiers who are bravely fighting to this day.

Table of Contents

We're Not OK

I originally created this as a visual compilation of
my emotions in October. Sadly, it's still the
reality for many of us. The Jewish people
have not had time to grieve. We are undergoing
immense psychological torture as self proclaimed
"activists" mock and gaslight us. I am drained.
Depressed. Angry. Losing sight of who I am.
My people are trapped in a living nightmare.
The terrorist propaganda has infected the west.
Their evil ideologies slowly form like cancer in the
minds of our youth. It's time to end this. We
deserve safety. We deserve healing. We deserve
freedom for our hostages. We deserve the protection
of our nation. This book is a collection of our voices.
It's time to listen- we are not okay.

Reflective Of The Year

So much to say with so much left to do.
This year has made me stronger with our
weaknesses exposed. I have become closer
to my family even though we still aren't that
close. I created through the pain. I've accepted
I'm popular, but not because of music & comedy,
although hopefully that'll change. I try to change
things that don't seem like they'll ever change,
but at least now y'all know my name.

- Rami Even-Esh | @koshadillz

Bring Them Home

I am frustrated, as I try to understand your pain.
I sometimes wish I could send you my energy- my entire
life force. It feels wrong to be drifting through life, as you
call out from underground. While the world slanders you,
I'm listening. I hear your silent screams. I feel it in every fiber
of my being. I am incomplete while you are gone. I will
continue to pray for you, even as unfamiliar as it may have
originally felt. I beg G-d to bring his children home. My
own screams are silenced from the tears blocking my
access to oxygen. But they are no match to the darkness
that has suffocated you. I have not forgotten. One day
we will heal together. As a people. As a nation.
As the children of G-d. Until then, I will
continue to shout- Bring Them Home Now!

- Rachelle Gage

Untitled

A pot boils over, spilling blood over the sides.

Bubbles like lives ended by the pop of a gun or a bomb.

And the world stirs the waters achingly slowly, the wooden

spoon is splintered like toothpicks to an open wound.

But those hands are rough and callous, and that

skin is not the skin that this water burns.

- Hana Tzipora

Be'eri

Bone-chilling dread,
as the masses chant words they
clearly do not understand.
"From the river... to the sea..." (Falastini, Arabi...)
If they knew, they wouldn't be saying it...
right?

An existential threat,
uttered from the mouths of many
blindfolded by the bandwagons
so artfully constructed and
camouflaged in the guise of
peace and freedom, "Intifada, Revolution."

Meanwhile, once again
we count our dead
we sift through the sand for
body parts, bone chips, and tefillin
to lay them to rest
never again?

I felt their screams as my own,
the tremble in their voices-
the anguish, rage, and fright.
Their bodies broken,
tortured and burned.
Mutilated, before the mercy of death.

Broadcast to the world
by terrorists who knew that
the scourge of gullible youth would cheer
them as they get away with murder.
Scurrying to hide under children's beds,
the monsters in the dark.

There is nothing new under the sun
for more than 3500 years.
We survived their armies at our gates.
Shema Y'israel, on our lips.
Baruch Hashem, in our minds.
Yerushalayim, in our bones.

- Elya Courtney

A House That Wasn't Mine

I was asked to house sit for a family friend with three kids, who
planned a vacation to Israel for Sukkot and Simchat Torah. I was
asleep in their house, when I got a message at midnight. It said
there were problems in Israel and things were worse than normal.
I turned off my phone and went back to sleep. I thought it was
just normal rockets. I thought everything would be fine.
It wasn't though.

I realized the next morning. I couldn't think on October 8th.
I forgot to eat or drink. I went to church and interpreted
the service into sign language. The pastor prayed for Israel
and I started crying. I couldn't stop. I left church feeling dead.
It took me over forty-eight hours to remember to drink.

The next month was a long nightmare. Coworkers tried to tell
me that Israel and Hamas were both equally bad, and that
the Middle East wasn't my problem, so I shouldn't be sad.
They didn't understand that I was in a house that wasn't mine.
Waiting for friends trapped overseas.

They didn't understand that one of my best friends is Israeli,
and that she sent me a goodbye message in October just
in case her family didn't survive. They didn't understand that
while I'm not Jewish, I've been to the Israel events.
I've been screamed at and had middle fingers directed at me,
and my picture taken without my consent.

In 2018 I visited a Synagogue to learn Hebrew.
I made friends and became involved in the community.
I've been more involved due to recent events.
I don't understand why the world is tolerating this hatred.

- Jewish ally, and friend, Ashley H.

On That Day

World I now present to you,
an atrocious & gruesome case.
Of evil depraved inhumanity;
torture, beheading & violent rape.

Crimes of frenzied insanity, recorded
as committed. Evidenced on GoPros,
acts obscene & purely wicked.

Horror, arson, mutilation. Whole families
burned alive. Mothers clutching babies,
smother them to survive.

Homes destroyed, ashes left, beyond
all recognition. Few survivors hidden
away, entire abolition.

Livestock perished, Earth on fire.
Devastated agriculture. Overseas
angels there to work, murdered
by this deadly vulture.

Step into the desert, a blissful
euphoric rise. Of a burning orange
sunshine, ascending from the sky.

Music, life, elation; celebrating love,
dance, peace & unity. Then BOOM from
up above, a massacre at a festival.

Rockets drop like hail from the
sky. Running in desperation,
hysterically trying to hide.

Laying on the ground, acting as
if dead, beside bodies of loved
ones, shot blank in the head.

Some run into bullets, desperate to
escape. The desert is vast & open,
they endure more brutal rape.

Roads are blocked, there's no way
out, every direction is a void. Masked
armed terrorists raging at large,
drug fuelled & overjoyed.

Cars burnt out, pure souls inside.
Metal carcasses litter the roads.
Bloodied bodies, limbs blown
off, taken in their loads.

Dragged by their hair, arms tied
back, a gunshot away from death.
Chaos, bedlam, anarchy.
Any moment their last breath.

Forced into Gaza, kidnapped
and paraded. Spat on, stamped on,
lured at. Barricaded, unaided, degraded.

Injured beyond imagination,
the streets they now ignite.
Sweet throwing celebrations, a
perverse, unfathomable delight.

World I ask your verdict, how do
you reply?...... "We don't believe
your evidence, we think it's all a lie."

"We believe you're all complicit,
we now wage our war on you.
We'll target & destroy you,
we'll turn on every single Jew."

"We'll march the streets, we'll
spread the hate, we'll tear
down hostage posters."

"We'll turn your world upside down,
You'll wish you'd never host us."

"We'll deny your pain, we'll damage
your goods. We'll graffiti on your doors.
We'll turn you into the wicked ones,
we'll be out in scores & scores."

"We'll rename it the resistance,
we'll call it freedom fighting. We'll
make you think you're going mad,
with off the scale gaslighting."

"We'll camp at universities, we'll
call it the occupation. We'll
damage the meaning of Zionist,
at every demonstration."

"We'll bombard social media, we'll
infiltrate your lives. We'll threaten
your very existence, we'll hope
you don't survive."

"We'll turn the world against you,
we'll make YOU the terrorist state.
We'll turn your truth into lies,
we'll make it legitimate."

"We'll shout you out of theatres,
we'll damage synagogues.
We'll intimidate you on the streets,
we'll change the dialogue."

"We'll fly the Palestinian flag,
we'll engage in no discussion.
We'll deface Jewish monuments,
they'll be no repercussion."

"We'll circulate propaganda,
we'll cover up our face. We'll
wear terror inspired headbands,
we'll annihilate your race."

"We'll make up genocidal slogans,
we'll chant them on the streets.
We'll make your city unbearable,
week
after
week
after
week."

-Rebecca Parker

Plea Of A Concerned Jewish Student

I am writing today to make my voice known as a Jewish student on your campus. I want the war to stop. I want the hostages freed, and innocent Israeli and Palestinian people to have full, beautiful, peaceful futures. In October, my cousin-in-law was shot in the neck by a Hamas terrorist in Israel and is still recovering. In January, my partner's childhood best friend was blown up and killed by a Hamas bomb at only 23 years old. Shani Louk, only a year older than myself, attended Portland Jewish Academy in kindergarten before she grew up to be captured, murdered, and have her corpse paraded around by terrorists. The pain of this war rings heavy through my home. Not a day has gone by where I have not wished it would end.

I have seen images of my university's library with signs out front calling to "Free Marwan Barghouti," a leader of the first and second intifada terror movements that rendered hundreds of Israeli civilians dead in the name of "revolution," and subsequently dubbing him the "Palestinian Nelson Mandela." "Genocide the Rich," "Blow up banks," "Globalize the Intifada," "AZAB (All Zionists Are Bastards)" are among some of the other slogans my school has been defaced with.

It is widely known Jews are stereotyped as wealthy or controlling banks. If you ask a self-proclaimed Zionist what that word actually means, it simply means we as Jews have a right to self-determination in our indigenous homeland, just as all indigenous people should, as echoed by the "land back" banners the protesters hang.

However, these protesters consider Jews illegitimate and deny
our indigeneity to any land outside of most often, "Poland",
where millions of my people were murdered for actually
NOT being considered European.

If we are to return to the diasporic countries, we resided in prior to
immigration to the US and Israel, most Israelis would be going back
to Iran, Morocco, and Iraq, where Jews remain few in numbers and
oppressed in devastating ways. Israelis who are Mizrahi or Sephardi
have ancestors who never left the Middle East - due to the irrefutable
fact we originate in the middle eastern land of Israel.

Personally, I am a first-generation student from a low income family,
raised in a single parent household held together at the seams by my
dad's social security disability checks. I am at Portland State for it's
"Transfers Finish Free" promise - however, despite the lack of a financial
burden, I find myself trying to finish my degree the opposite of free,
as I carry an extremely distressing emotional and mental burden,
and fear for my physical safety.

My ancestors immigrated to North America undocumented
from the USSR, narrowly escaping the imminent genocide
Eastern European Jews of the 20th century were faced with.
They sought a better life free of persecution. I am sad to say
that the ancient hatred my ancestors sought to flee
has caught up with their descendants.

I come to you today as a descendent of the less than half
of Jewish people who remained alive before 1938 and after 1942.
I do not want to hide my Star of David necklace, my heritage, or
my religion in the year 2024. I do not want to have to avoid campus.
But my safety is contingent on all of these factors as long as these
"protests" are allowed and embraced as "passionate free speech."

To assume good intent with these "protestors" may feel okay
for those without a connection to the conflict, but for me, it would
be gaslighting myself and puts me in direct danger. Based on the
above quotes from the banners in the "liberated zone" and the
property destruction on our campus, it is safe to say these people
are not anti-war peace mongers; these are terror embracing
insurrectionists. I can assure you if I sought to join their movement
as a student who embraced peace, I would be laughed out of their
"liberated zone." Peace is the antithesis of their cause.

To put it plainly, I am disheartened and demoralized by the university's drawn-out efforts to negotiate with students who endorse terror and the delegitimization of calls for destruction of my homeland. What a strange experience, to sit at home for two days while my campus is closed because people who hate me have demands that are being negotiated with, and who's hatred has so far been met with no tangible repercussions.

The precedent this sets has solidified for me that I will not be applying to a Graduate program at Portland State next year, SPECIFICALLY the school of Social Work who has seemingly been allowed to publicly take a stance on the situation and hold one sided racist teach-ins (yes, antisemitism is racism), simply out of fear for my safety and no evidence of protections for Jewish students like myself who holds her freedom of self determination dear. I hope to see our campus grounds safe and clean as soon as possible.

- Anonymous Student, "Kendall"
Bachelor of Science in Psychology Track
Portland State University

Never Erased

As the world attempts to tear you from existence,
scrutinizing your experiences, I mark your torn posters
with my prayers. "The pen is mightier than the sword,"
they say; I hope this is true as I write my poems for you.
You'll never be forgotten, as you are in the hearts and
minds of the Jewish people. You are our family, and
we will not desert you. I continually think about you,
on my way to and from work, armed with a sharpie in
my purse. For when the wicked try to tear you down,
I spread my message for you- never forget, never again.

- Rachelle Gage

The Invisible Star

In Judaism, life is valued at the highest level.
Saving one life is like saving an entire world. The
Jewish Star represents this, and is worn as an amulet.
Since October 7th, it has been very difficult to wear
this emblem in public, as it could put one's life in danger.
The ability to instead take this symbol and engrave it in your
heart and internalize it, is more important. If you have to
hide your Star to save your life, just know it is not invisible,
but is visible in our hearts.

- Concerned Jewish Mother

Peace Desert

The first image the algorithm
chose to break the news, was a
bloody teenage girl being dragged
by her hair and begging for rescue.

A day that was supposed to be of rest
and joy became one of doom-scrolling.
Technological feeds overflowing with
fresh records of brutality.

Clips of families desperately trying
to stay hidden, hoping that their
shelter isn't set ablaze or that their
door doesn't give way.

Displays of broken young people
whose bodies were defiled after death
and paraded throughout the streets.

Wonder if their loved ones even
knew they had been enjoying music
at the wrong place and time.

Echos of young children asking their
mother for reassurance that they'll
be okay, as their kidnappers shove
them to the ground.

The callousness in the comments ask
what did the parents expect when
they gave birth in that particular country.

The celebration of people
whose existence has been deemed
problematic were now being cut short.

The promises that this will be
globalized, to teach the Jews to
stay in their place, which can only
be reasonably concluded as nowhere.

Wondering if the mother clutching her
infants was kept safe as her captors
promised in the video they released to
give plausible deniability to the atrocities.

None of this is unexpected in an
environment where any affiliation
to the tribe elicits purity tests.

According to the commenters,
these are supposedly what the other
side faces daily, so it is justified.

The agreed-upon narrative by those
cheering on the uprising against the
supposed colonizers conveniently
ignores the attempts at peace
negations and treaties.

Or that both groups have historical
and indigenous ties to the land.

The Overton window seems to
have widened to allow the calls
to bring back gas chambers
and the final solution.

The calls for genocide are
conditioned as socially acceptable
as long as they are painted under
the concern for another group.

Aren't we supposed to root for the underdog?

There is a familiar degradation of trying
to find out if dear ones are safe only to
have to scroll past self-righteous lectures by
those with the luxury of being on the outside;
who often have a limited understanding
of the geopolitics or history.

Sleep eludes as the horrors have been
seared to the mind. Knowing that this
is just seen as a cycle of violence,
any defense will be vilified.

That depends on who you talk to, the
humanity of one group has been erased.
The world has helped to create this
peace desert and is eager to turn its eye.

For it's always been far easier just to blame the Jews.

- A.S. Banks

UNholy

The world wages war: But where's your
uproar? UNsure, you ignore, and make her
the whore. You support the violator,
scheming woman hater. Screaming 'til
your face turns bluish, she's ignored,
because she is: Jewish?

Is your memory hazy? 'Cause she's Israeli?
Degraded and paraded. Choked and
provoked. UNwoke. Her dignity gone.
I'm wailing it's wrong. Your failing is strong.

You haven't spoken. Her pelvis is broken.
You think she deserved it? This is disturbed shit.
She's UNstable. Can't walk. While you're
UNable, to talk.

Do you align with the bully? It's online,
FULLY. You decline. The insanity, war is
catastrophe. UNhumanity. Weaponising
words, neologists arriving in herds. Terror
apologists, brainless and bland. While
weak men waste their seed on a land.

HOLY?
No holiness here. Just violated
holes bleeding. Isolated souls speaking.
Weeping, begging for death. We remain
deaf to each other, blinded by the tribal.
Violence is a cycle.

Ancient rivalry, more than binary.
Bribery, corruption, derisory eruption.
We are all blended, UNfriended.
Lives ended. Why? What for?

Does she lie? Shot in her bed, locked
in her head. Covered in rubble. Smothered,
in a tunnel. The truth is vile by media trial.
So feed her large doses of DENIAL.

Rape her, bugger her. Don't forget
to drug her. Darkness; whisper.
Stillness now, sister. She sees only black.
He's now come back. Don't ask.
UNseen. UNmask; it's green.

Ancient memory, from the last century.
Here's the hitter, revenge is... bitter.
Stick it on Twitter. Sorry, X. He wants sex,
with a dead child. It's wild. 'Cause it'll be denied,
even with footage of blood from the backside.

G-d forbid a military force reaction. They raped
a Yid, you merrily endorse this faction. UNkind
and UNgentle. You praise the fUNdemental.

Depraved at a rave. You revel at the devil.
Dialling backwards? Defiling a kibbutz?
Context is nonsense, there is no context.

For this Jew cancelling concept, a contest
of specifics? The victims' Olympics.
Criminal, UNlivable, UNforgivable.
A flood of blood money RUNNING.

Raiders of our future prophets.
While leaders made fortunes from
futures' profits. Prayed for aid.
She's still afraid. How many days?
You still UNswayed?

Maybe she'll adapt? Baby kidnapped. Post
truth. You remain aloof. Without proof. Further
investigates? You say she exaggerates? I'm
watching & wincing. But for you, UNconvincing.
Antisemitism epidemic. Intellectual, academic.

Destruction, abduction, and rape. ILLEGAL.
You celebrate and desecrate my people.
Everything is senseless. Do we remain
defenceless? Dead children, consequences.
Enemies sniped out, families wiped out.

The transgressor is the oppressor. The
oppressor is the transgressor. Don't be
deceived. The aggressor is the aggrieved.
How dare we be conceived?

Confused? By all the words that are used?
Abused? There is no lingua franca.
Just lies; propaganda. Reported, but
distorted. From the river to the sea;
You're a Hitler wannabe.

The timing amplified, by rhyming genocide.
The news not bona fide, and yet I'm petrified of
another link. Draconian, dystopian, doublethink.
Delegitimise my state. Dehumanise my fate.
Normalise your hate. Formalise your fight.

Keep being cruel. Send your kids to killing
school. Waking fascism, faking activism. UNcool.
Hope and love must make me the fool. Hysteric
fright. You won't crush me with barbaric might.
Cause I'll rush in with esoteric light.

I'll push in with exoteric flight. As I welcome
the Festival of Light. An aura, my menorah.
Meditation, no more miseducation. Causing
a conflation. Just Anti Zion?

I'm not buying. I am anti dying. While Jew
hate is simply flying off the shelves, we're
murdering ourselves. You bored of me crying?
You prefer my silence?

If you defer on sexual violence, I don't need
your approval. UNrepenting removal.

So, is this the beginning of the end? Again.
Where all the Jews are condemned? Again.
Welcome to the sequels. Worldwide hatred
equals a unified and sacred people.

You dejected me, rejected me. So
unexpectedly or predictably, (irony of
ironies), the only place that offers to
protect me with love; you UNderstand?
Is that scapegoated slab;
The holy land.

- Debra Tammer

Eyes On The Lies

Are your eyes fixed on the east?
Wondering why there's no peace?
Hostages were kidnapped and buried alive.
Their stories forgotten because of a lie.

As our eyes turn to Rafah, we see
hundreds of hostages forced to stay.
Their lives fading away day by day.
People like us buried alive.
Pain ignored because of a lie.

The children are dying alone they say.
They should be eating watermelon this May.
Do you see the Americans buried alive?
Or quietly ignore them to scream genocide?

Rafah's on fire! The people are dying!
Were they blind in October when we were crying?
We remember our hostages buried alive.
Their screams silenced by a terrible lie.

Do all eyes on Rafah not see why
Hamas forces must flee? Hostages taken,
families obliterated, women raped. These
innocent hostages still haven't escaped.

They've been buried alive.
Their pain erased by a lie.

Are you still asking why there's not peace?
The answer lies buried beneath the surface.
Terrorists are not a resistance resurgence.
With hostages captured and buried alive.
Hamas support grows because of their lies.

But we see the hostages buried alive.
We'll never forget them despite the lies.

So keep all eyes on Rafah,
and all blame on Hamas.
Tell them we want Kfir Bibas.

We speak up for the hostages buried alive.
We never forget for we don't believe lies.

- Jewish ally, and friend, Ashley H.

We Are Not The Same

We sing for peace.
You chant for death and destruction.

We build, communities, businesses, and ideas.
You bulldoze greenhouses and work to dismantle
the very universities that allow you to feel
empowered enough to act like useful idiots.

We contribute to society.
You poison minds with baseless
propaganda and straight up lies.

We value life.
You value death.

We have had the same identity, religion,
and traditions throughout our history.
You shape shift to fit the narrative of
the day, now painting yourselves as
an oppressed minority group in the
Muslim-majority Middle East.

We embrace diversity.
You demand complete
uniformity and punish dissent.

We bring light.
You shroud the world in darkness.

We encourage
education and debate.
You only teach
propaganda and hate.

We are indigenous.
You are not.

Yet, we have offered to share
the land, time and again, and
you have rejected our offers,
time and again.

We are survivors.
Time will tell what you are.
If history is any indication...

Oh right, you don't read

- JEWishly

Lucky You

Lucky you, not glued to the news. No
urgency to flee, because you're a Jew.
Your fears are not deemed hysteria, no
need for extra protection in your area.

You're entertained by the dress up
terrorists, only maddened by their arrests.
Always believed that you're a minority,
your hate crimes automatically a priority.

No one glorifies your executioners,
instead they're considered revolutioners.
Your slurs are off limits. If someone dares
slander you, they're cancelled in minutes.

Today's hoods aren't white, but still
symbolize terror, death, and spite.
No need to reroute or replan, your
memorials are sacred, haters are banned.

Permission to protest, spreading false
news and libels. It's all a game,
like sports team rivals.

Thinking you're valid, seen as a righteous
voice of the oppressed. While demeaning
the victim, in every possible way-
you're truly obsessed.

Creating false identities, siding with savages.
Clearly 3500 years of history is only our baggage.
So please, continue your dissonance.
You'll simply be remembered for your ignorance.

Associated with actual Nazis, for your
hidden bias. But no one will ostracize you,
you're moral and pious.

Why would you care for the fate of the Jews?
To be so naive, lucky you.

- Rachelle Gage

Nice Jewish Runners

On October 7th, Sderot Front Runners tragically lost four of their runners to the brutal terrorist attacks in Israel. There was silence from a lot of people in the running community, and a lot of my friends felt the same. Everyone was looking for ways to show support. Runners love to come together, so I wrote a simple Instagram post- how about we do a run together?

That eventually turned into our own running club with its own Instagram page. The community was very involved in starting this up from the beginning, from a member creating our logo to people participating in an online poll to express interest, and later come up with the group name. It was obvious that this was something a lot of people needed at the time.

Do we want to be running as a group of Jewish people?
Do we want to be a target? Should we be afraid?

Months later, this beautiful community has grown exponentially, with hundreds of members joining each week. We have sold more than 250 sweatshirts, hundreds of shirts, as well as various other products with our logo, which has the Star of David. Our group has expanded to 19 cities worldwide, including Tel Aviv and Toronto. This club has helped a lot of us go from being afraid to proudly expressing our Judaism.

- Ezra Feig

One Year

Today marks a year since that horrific day,
October 7th.
Out of the darkness, we will rise from the ashes, like
a phoenix. Am Yisrael Chai, the people of Israel live.
Reborn from the embers of despair, our spirits
intertwined in a vibrant tapestry of hope.

Repairing the world is etched deep in our souls,
as we gather the shattered fragments of history.
The glass of our past, each shard tells a story. A
story of resilience, a story of strength. The furnace
of hatred we endured. We will never forget.

With each heartbeat, we carry the memories of
our people. Standing in our power and legacy of
those before us, their voices resonate in the silence.
Angels watching over us from the heavens —
may they lead us into a better world, a world to BE.

The numbers roll by, too many lost without names.
Their faces imprinted on our hearts, a constellation
of hope amid the darkness, illuminating the path as
we honor their light. On October 7th, we remember
their lives, each soul a flickering candle
in the shadow of hatred.

We stand united, weaving a quilt of resilience.
Binding our wounds, fortifying our resolve.
As we rise, we bear the weight of our ancestors'
dreams- a promise to never forget, to
transform grief into action.

From this pain, we will share our light. A
testament to love, unity, and the power of our
story. Out of the darkness, we rise-our duty, our
calling. Tikkun Olam is engraved in our soul.

Lo Bashamayim Hi. It is not in heaven, but
here, in our hands, we hold the power to repair,
to rise, to restore. We pray. I pray. We pray.

Chazak, Chazak, V'nitchazeik-
Be strong, and let us strengthen one another.
The remaining souls, held hostage for almost a year-
Bring them home.
NOW.
ALIVE.

- Tikkunelana

October 7th And Beyond

From safety to surprise.
From insecurity to blessings, or not.
Wondering about a plan,
or if the plan has survived.

What do I tell the children?
What do I tell myself?
How can I continue to stroll through life?

Knowing that my enemy's plan survives,
the beastiality of their actions.
Yet, they accuse me of anti-Zionism.
The world is topsy-turvy,
with no rhyme or rhythm.

Friends are enemies,
and enemies may be friends.
The truth is scorned.
The Israeli victims not embraced
Am I ok? No.

But not victimized. Lincoln said,
"We must be truthful and fair in
our ordinary affairs of life."
"We must be truthful and fair in
our patriotism and religion."

The enemy strolls through life,
with his friends bloodying
us and more. We must rise up
and feel his power of truth,
the power to overcome.

We are not helpless,
we are empowered.
Hashem will be the wind
beneath our wings,
to overcome.

- Larry Marks

Acknowledgements

I would like to extend a heartfelt thank you to all
of the authors who submitted a piece for this book. I took
a chance sharing this idea on social media, reaching out
in Facebook groups and posting on Instagram stories.
My digital calling could have easily been ignored
in the vast sea of online content.

Instead, I was contacted by those with similar
sentiments. Other voices who felt silenced. Scared.
Depressed. Simply put, they were also not OK.

I am honored to raise these voices. To create this
visual archive of our perspectives. I would also
like to acknowledge all those who have vigorously
fought against antisemitism, as well as those who
have continually advocated for the nation of Israel.

I am proud to say that while we are not OK,
we are certainly not alone.